DEPARTMENT OF THE NAVY
HEADQUARTERS UNITED STATES MARINE CORPS
3000 MARINE CORPS PENTAGON
WASHINGTON, DC 20350-3000

ACTIVE DUTY FOR OPERATIONAL SUPPORT (ADOS) IN SUPPORT OF THE TOTAL FORCE

DEPARTMENT OF THE NAVY
HEADQUARTERS UNITED STATES MARINE CORPS
3000 MARINE CORPS PENTAGON
WASHINGTON, DC 20350-3000

MCO 1001.59A
RAP
19 JAN 2011

MARINE CORPS ORDER 1001.59A

From: Commandant of the Marine Corps
To: Distribution List

Subj: ACTIVE DUTY FOR OPERATIONAL SUPPORT (ADOS) IN SUPPORT OF THE TOTAL FORCE (SHORT TITLE: ADOS)

Ref: (a) 10 U.S.C. § 115, 10211, 12301(a), (b), (d), 12302, 12304, 12310, 12686, 12731, Chapter 1607
     (b) DOD Instruction 1215.06, "Uniform Reserve, Training, and Retirement Categories," December 24, 2008
     (c) MCO 1800.11
     (d) DOD Instruction 7730.54, "Reserve Component Common Personnel Data System (RCCPDS)," July 28, 2010
     (e) NAVSO P-6034
     (f) MCO P3000.19A
     (g) MCO P1900.16F
     (h) MCO 1001R.1K
     (i) NAVMED P-117
     (j) MCO 6110.3
     (k) MCO 5000.12E
     (l) MCO 1001.61,
     (m) Marine Corps Total Force System Personnel Reporting Instructions Users Manual (MCTFSPRIUM)
     (n) DOD 7000.14-R, "Department of Defense Financial Management Regulations (FMR)," Date varies by Volume (Various Volumes)
     (o) MCO P1610.7F)
     (p) MCO P1070.12K
     (q) SECNAVINST 1770.3D
     (r) JAGINST 5800.7E, "Manual of the Judge Advocate General," June 20, 2007
     (s) TRICARE Policy Manual 6010.57M
     (t) 10 U.S.C. Subtitle A, Part II, Chapter 47
     (u) MCO 1050.3J
     (v) SECNAV M-5210.1

Encl: (1) Definitions
      (2) ADOS Personnel Eligibility Requirements
      (3) Program Administration
      (4) ADOS Budget Working Group
      (5) ADOS Categories and Component Codes

DISTRIBUTION STATEMENT A: Approved for public release; distribution is unlimited.

1. <u>Situation</u>. The Active Duty for Operational Support (ADOS) program provides Marine Corps Reserve personnel augmentation for both Active and Reserve components, in support of existing and emerging requirements of the Marine Corps Total Force to meet short-term administrative, operational, and exercise support requirements.

    a. The purpose of this order is to delineate governing policies and procedures required to employ Marines using the ADOS program.

    b. Reference (a), Section 12301(d), provides statutory authority to order Reserve Component (RC) members, with their consent, to active duty (AD).

2. <u>Cancellation</u>. MCO 1001.59.

3. <u>Mission</u>. This order establishes policies and procedures for the authorized assignment of RC personnel to AD under the ADOS Program per references (a) through (v).

4. <u>Execution</u>

    a. <u>Commander's Intent</u>

        (1) Provide Marine Corps Reserve personnel augmentation of appropriate grade and skills to both Active and Reserve components, in support of existing and emerging requirements of the Marine Corps Total Force, to meet short-term administrative, operational, and exercise support requirements. Short-term is defined as:

            (a) One-year or less for conventional ADOS.

            (b) Three-years or less for Contingency Operations ADOS.

        (2) Prevent unintended impacts of statutory restrictions and position the Marine Corps to meet future mission requirements through judicious employment and effective management of Reserve manpower.

            (a) ADOS is intended to accomplish those specific duties required to complete the operational, administrative or exercise support requirements identified on each orders request.

            (b) The ADOS program is not intended to overcome existing or recurring T/O sourcing shortfalls.

            (c) Commanders must carefully consider the total cost of ADOS orders. Particular attention must be made towards reducing per diem requirements by locally sourcing staffing needs when possible.

            (d) As a volunteer program, Marines serving on ADOS may terminate orders by providing at least two weeks notice; likewise Commanders may terminate a Marine's ADOS orders provided that the Marine is given at least two weeks notice.

b. Concept of Operations

(1) The ADOS program replaces the program formerly known as Active Duty for Special Work (ADSW) and is managed by Director, Reserve Affairs (RA) Division, Manpower and Reserve Affairs (M&RA), Headquarters Marine Corps (HQMC).

(2) Reference (b) defines ADOS as authorized voluntary AD for RC personnel, other than Active Reserve (AR) duty pursuant to section 12301(d) of reference (a).

(3) ADOS categories are determined by two funding sources, Military Personnel, Marine Corps (MPMC) for ADOS-Active Component (ADOS-AC) or Reserve Personnel, Marine Corps (RPMC) for ADOS-Reserve Component (ADOS-RC).

(4) A third category, ADOS-Contingency Operations (ADOS-CO), is a subset of ADOS-AC controlled by Manpower Management Force Augmentation (MMFA) Branch, Manpower Management (MM) Division, M&RA.

(5) Conventional ADOS funding is a discretionary budget item within the MPMC and RPMC appropriations. Funding is allocated by Deputy Commandant, Programs and Resources (DC P&R) to Director, RA for prioritization and distribution to ADOS Operational Sponsors (OpSponsors). The OpSponsors subsequently allocate funding to corresponding Gaining Force Commanders (GFCs) or other requesting agencies for non ADOS-CO orders.

(6) ADOS-CO is a discretionary budget item within the MPMC appropriations and is allocated by DC P&R to Director, MM (funding is based on existing operational requirements and managed by MMFA).

(7) The category of ADOS funding is determined by the primary beneficiary of the majority of work to be performed by the member (i.e. ADOS-AC is the funding source when the majority of work is performed for the AC, while ADOS-RC is used if the majority of work is performed for the RC).

(8) Accordingly, the funding source used determines the component against which the billet counts for end strength accounting purposes when a Marine exceeds 1095 days within a 1460 day period.

(9) To assist the Marine Corps Total Force and Requesting Agencies, the following criteria are provided:

(a) The requirement for ADOS should be temporary in nature with a clearly defined termination date.

(b) Marines assigned to duty under ADOS should possess the appropriate Military Occupational Specialty (MOS) or civilian skills necessary to accomplish the mission.

(c) Conventional ADOS will not be funded for greater than 365 days without written approval by Director, RA.

<u>1</u>. Marines may request orders via a Gaining Force Commander (GFC).

<u>2</u>. A GFC has the authority to issue orders for up to 365 days, within the ADOS budget approved by the respective Operational Sponsor and Director, RA.

<u>3</u>. Per enclosure (2), requests to extend authorized duty beyond 365 days or provide for consecutive periods of duty exceeding 365 days require written approval from the Director, RA.

(d) Marines on ADOS may not exceed 1,095 days within the preceding 1,460 days without prior approval of Director, RA.

(e) Per reference (c), Marines may not be assigned ADOS beyond 16 years of AD without prior approval of Deputy Commandant, Manpower and Reserve Affairs (DC M&RA).

(f) With the exception of ADOS-CO, ADOS shall not be performed in a areas subject to hostile fire or imminent danger pay without prior approval of the Director, RA.

(g) Marines performing ADOS are subject to the requirements of enclosure (2).

c. <u>Subordinate Element Missions</u>

(1) <u>DC M&RA</u>

(a) <u>Director, Manpower Information Systems Division (MI)</u>

<u>1</u>. Implement automated solutions for identifying, tracking and reporting all Marines, regardless of funding source for orders, who are on ADOS.

<u>2</u>. Provide automated solutions for identifying, tracking, reporting, and forecasting all Marines, regardless of funding source for orders, those personnel on ADOS orders that will cross the threshold of 1,095 days of AD within 1,460 days.

<u>3</u>. Support adjacent agencies within M&RA with the capability to generate reports on AC and AR end strength.

(b) <u>Director, Manpower Management Division (MM)</u>

<u>1</u>. Manage and adjudicate requests for ADOS-CO, to include permanent change of station orders (PCSO) if mission and operational requirements justify the issuance of ADOS-CO PCSO.

<u>2</u>. Provide guidance concerning permanent change of station decisions in conjunction with ADOS orders.

<u>3</u>. Manage and track PCS authorizations for ADOS-AC and ADOS-CO.

<u>4</u>. Manage the per diem authority in accordance with reference (e) and current service policies.

<u>5</u>. Track joint Reserve augmentation requirements for current contingency operations.

(c) <u>Director, Manpower Plans and Policy (MP)</u>

<u>1</u>. In coordination with Director, RA and Deputy Commandant, Plans, Policies, and Operations (DC PP&O), publish Total Force manpower guidance governing the validation, sourcing, and administration of ADOS-CO joint manpower requirements.

<u>2</u>. In accordance with section 115 of reference (a) and reference (d), report to DC M&RA and DC P&R those personnel on ADOS-AC that exceed 1,095 days within the preceding 1,460 days and count against AC end strength.

<u>3</u>. Provide monthly execution data for ADOS-AC orders.

(d) <u>Director, RA</u>

<u>1</u>. Develop ADOS policy, maintain and administer the ADOS Order, and provide program execution oversight.

<u>2</u>. Screen requests for ADOS that enable a Marine to accumulate more than 16 years AD in accordance with reference (c).

<u>3</u>. In accordance with section 115 of reference (a) and reference (d), report to DC M&RA and DC P&R those personnel on ADOS-RC that exceed 1,095 days within the preceding 1,460 days and count against AR end strength.

<u>4</u>. Convene the ADOS Budget Working Group (ABWG) annually to formulate and prioritize ADOS mid-year review and next fiscal year (FY) funding requirements.

<u>5</u>. Based on the ABWG and annual President Budget, finalize and publish ADOS funding allocations.

<u>6</u>. In accordance with reference (d), prepare and

forward required monthly manpower reports to Office of the Assistant Secretary of Defense, Reserve Affairs (OASD/RA).

(2) Deputy Commandant, Programs and Resources (P&R)

(a) Maintain oversight of Resource Management Decisions (RMDs) from the Department of the Navy or Office of the Secretary of Defense affecting ADOS appropriations and provide that information to Director, RA Division.

(b) Provide information to the Director, RA on funding levels for year of execution in all ADOS categories and provide updates as required.

(c) Provide funding controls for ADOS-RC Permanent Change of Station (PCS) authorizations.

(3) Marine Corps Total Force and other Requesting Agencies

(a) Ensure that ADOS orders are issued in compliance with this order, using enclosures (2) and (3) for command screening requirements and sponsorship - at no time should a Marine be authorized or directed to report for a period of AD without a set of authenticated orders for the period.

(b) In accordance with reference (f), provide administrative and support functions to Marines reporting for ADOS prior to commencing duty with the gaining command and again prior to departing the gaining command's location for the Marine's home or parent command.

(c) Ensure Marines on ADOS who deploy overseas receive all applicable entitlements. Conduct audits upon deployment and redeployment to ensure such entitlements start and stop on time.

(d) Ensure all Marines meet pre-deployment training requirements for overseas ADOS assignments.

(e) Ensure RC Marines on ADOS in excess of 30 days have a current medical screening or physical prior to release from AD per enclosure (3).

(f) Submit NAVMC 11349 forms with justification for ADOS funding to Director, RA during the second quarter of each FY NLT the date prescribed in the ABWG convening MARADMIN published annually per enclosure (4).

(4) OpSponsors. Ensure commands request and utilize ADOS in compliance with this order.

5. Administration and Logistics

a.   Recommendations concerning the contents of this Order may be forwarded to Director, RA via the appropriate chain of command.

b.   Records created as a result of this directive shall include records management requirements to ensure the proper maintenance and use of records, regardless of format or medium, to promote accessibility and authorized retention per the approved records schedule and reference (v).

6. Command and Signal

a.   Command. This Order is applicable to the Marine Corps Total Force.

b.   Signal. This Order is effective the date signed.

R. E. MILSTEAD JR
Deputy Commandant for
Manpower and Reserve Affairs

DISTRIBUTION: PCN 10200136600

Definitions

1. <u>Active Duty (AD)</u>. Full-time duty in the active military service of the United States. It includes full-time training, annual training duty, and attendance, while in active military service, at a school designated as a service school by law or by the Secretary of the military department concerned.

2. <u>Active Duty for Operational Support (ADOS)</u>. A category of voluntary AD used to provide RC support to operations and mission requirements. It includes AD, other than AR duty pursuant to section 12301(d) of reference (a) and AD for training performed at the request of an organizational or operational commander or as a result of reimbursable funding. It does not include annual training (AT), Reserve Counterpart Training (RCT), attendance at professional military education (PME), or other categories of Active Duty for Training (ADT).

3. <u>Active Duty for Training (ADT)</u>. A category of AD used to provide structured individual training, unit training, or educational courses to RC members. Included in the ADT category are AT, Initial Active Duty for Training (IADT), and Other Training Duty (OTD).

4. <u>Active Duty Other Than for Training (ADOT)</u>. A category of AD used to provide RC support to either AC or RC missions. It includes categories of ADOS, AR duty, and involuntary AD pursuant to sections 12301, 12302, and 12304 of reference (a). Training may occur in the conduct of ADOT.

5. <u>Active Reserve (AR)</u>. Marines who are part of the Selected Marine Corps Reserve (SMCR) on full-time duty under 10 U.S.C. Section 12301(d) pursuant to the AD described in sections 101(d), 10211, and 12310 of reference (a) for the purpose of organizing, administering, recruiting, instructing, or training the RC.

6. <u>Annual Training (AT)</u>. A category of AD used to provide individual and/or unit readiness training. SMCR members must perform a minimum period of training each year to satisfy Marine Corps training requirements associated with their assignment. AT may also be used to provide operational or administrative support of AC missions and requirements, when its primary purpose of individual and/or unit readiness training is simultaneously accomplished.

7. <u>Cumulative Active Service</u>. The total amount of active service a Marine has accumulated on AD.

8. <u>End Strength</u>. The authorized personnel strength set by Congress each FY for AC and RC personnel.

9. <u>Gaining Force Command (GFC)</u>. This command is the unit to which the Marine is joined for performing ADOS. It is directly responsible

for unit diary entries, administrative support, assistance, and sponsorship of the member.

10. Individual Mobilization Augmentee (IMA). An individual member of the SMCR who receives training and is pre-assigned to fill individual military billets which augment active component structure and missions of the Marine Corps, Department of Defense and other departments or agencies of the U.S. Government to meet requirements of the organization to support mobilization requirements, contingency operations, or other specialized or technical requirements.

11. Individual Ready Reserve (IRR). A pre-trained manpower pool of Ready Reservists who are not in the SMCR. The IRR consists of (1) Marines who have had training and served previously in the AC or in the SMCR and have some period of Military Service Obligation (MSO) remaining, (2) Marines who have completed their MSO and are in the IRR by choice, and (3) Marines on the Delayed Entry Program.

12. Military Personnel, Marine Corps (MPMC). An appropriation category used to fund activities that support the AC.

13. Mobilization Training Unit (MTU). A unit established to provide RC training in a non-pay status for volunteers of the IRR and the Standby Reserve (Active Status List) attached under competent authority and participating in such units for retirement points.

14. Operation and Maintenance, Marine Corps (O&MMC). An appropriation category used to fund activities that support the AC.

15. Ready Reserve. The Ready Reserve is comprised of military members of the Reserve, organized in units or as individuals, or both, and liable for involuntary order to AD in time of war or national emergency under reference (a). The Ready Reserve of the Marine Corps consists of the SMCR and the IRR.

16. Reserve Counterpart Training (RCT). A program designed to give members of the IRR (Majors and below for officers; Gunnery Sergeants and below for enlisted Marines) an opportunity to enhance military skills by training with their AC counterparts. RCT provides mobilization readiness training for pre-assigned IRR Marines.

17. Reserve Personnel, Marine Corps (RPMC). An appropriation category used to fund activities that support the RC.

18. Selected Marine Corps Reserve (SMCR). That portion of the Ready Reserve consisting of members of units, IMAs, individuals serving on the AR program and members performing IADT.

19. Theater Security Cooperation (TSC). Those activities the CCDRs conduct within their AOR in order to promote official and unofficial relations between the U.S. military and foreign governments,

international organizations, industries, and people of other nations aimed at furthering U.S. national security interests and promoting U.S. values abroad. ADOS orders in support of TSC fall into the ADOS AC category. MPMC funding for pay and allowances is provided by the Traditional CCDR Activities (TCA) Operational Sponsor, while O&MMC travel and per diem costs are CCDR funded via direct site fund data.

ADOS Personnel Eligibility Requirements

1. **General**. This enclosure provides detailed information on the policy, authority, and overarching procedures, and effects associated with the management of RC personnel serving on ADOS.

2. **Background**. Section 12301(d) of reference (a) provides for orders to AD for RC members with the consent of those members, contingent on the limits established in Section 115 and the protection of Section 12686 of reference (a).

   a. Those members on ADOS orders that exceed 1095 days in a 1460-day period count towards the annual authorizations for the AC or AR personnel end strength.

   b. Prudent and effective management of Reserve manpower will prevent unintended impacts of statutory restrictions and position the Marine Corps to meet future mission requirements.

3. **Policy**

   a. Permission for AD service by a RC member beyond 16 years of AD is granted in accordance with reference (c).

   b. ADOS orders resulting in a Marine counting against AC end strength must be approved by the Director, MP.

   c. ADOS orders resulting in a Marine counting against AR end strength must be approved by the Director, RA.

   d. ADOS orders will not result in a member exceeding five years of continuous AD (separations pay criteria is six years) without the approval of the Director, MP for MPMC funded orders or the Director, RA for RPMC funded orders.

   e. ADOS orders will not exceed 365 days of continuous service without the approval of the Director, RA unless the orders are in support of a contingency operation and approved by MMFA.

   f. AD service with breaks of 30 days or less is considered continuous AD service.

4. **Computation of Cumulative AD**

   a. In order to determine the total number of AD years the Marine will possess at the end of a requested set of orders, commands will add the number of days ADOS being requested to the total number of AD points resident on the Career Retirement Credit Report (CRCR) and divide this total by 365.
   (TOTAL AD POINTS + CURRENT ORDERS [INCLUSIVE]/365) = ACDU YEARS

b.   Per references (b) and (c), this method is the approved formula for computation of cumulative AD under this Order.

5.   End Strength Exclusions

a.   As previously stipulated, those members exceeding the aforementioned statutory limits count towards AC or AR end strength.

b.   However, the following periods of AD are excluded from counting towards the 1095 days:

(1) Active Duty for Training (ADT).

(2) Periods of involuntary AD under Sections 12301(a), 12301(b), 12302, and 12304 of reference (a).

(3) Prior service in the AC.

c.   Marines serving on orders that specify a period greater than 1095 days in a 1460-day period shall be immediately included in AC or AR end strength accounting.

d.   The cumulative number of Marines serving on ADOS above the number annually authorized by Congress shall count against AC or AR end strength based on the funding source (MPMC or RPMC respectively).

e.   Commands requesting conventional ADOS orders which will result in a Marine exceeding 1095 days of AD in a 1460-day period are required to submit written justification to Director, RA NLT 60 days prior to the effective date of the orders.

f.   Commands requesting ADOS-CO orders which will result in a Marine exceeding 1095 days of AD in a 1460-day period are required to submit justification to Director, MM (MMFA) via the Marine Corps Mobilization Processing System NLT 60 days prior to the effective date of the orders.

6.   Medical

a.   Prior to acceptance and initiation of ADOS orders, Marines must be physically fit for duty in accordance with references (h), (i) and (j).

b.   The member's medical records will be screened by an appropriate medical department representative (MDR) prior to issuing orders.

c.   The MDR will determine the type of medical assessment required in accordance with reference (i).

d. Members may contact their MDR, unit corpsman, local military medical facility, authorized provider, or administrative command for assistance.

e. Acceptable forms of documentation for physical fitness include a Preventive Health Assessment (PHA) completed within the last year and documented in the Medical Readiness Reporting System (MRRS).

f. If a PHA has not been completed within the last year, the following forms of documentation are also acceptable:

(1) Form DD 2807-1, "Report of Medical History", completed within the last six months if separated from AD service or SMCR within the last two years, or

(2) A complete physical examination completed within the last six months if separated from AD service or the last two years if separated from the SMCR.

g. Marines in the IRR may be brought on ADOS orders without the documentation required in paragraph 6.a. but must complete a PHA, or other approved form of documentation, within ten days of the commencement date of the period of ADOS.

h. Per reference (h), an HIV test must be conducted within 12 months of executing ADOS orders of 30 days or more and entered in the Marine Corps Total Force System (MCTFS).

i. Pregnant Marines desiring to perform ADOS must comply with the provisions contained in reference (k).

7. Physical Fitness

a. SMCR Marines who request to perform ADOS must meet Marine Corps height and weight standards and the physical fitness requirements of reference (j), or have already been assigned to the Body Composition Program (BCP), prior to receiving orders.

b. IRR Marines receiving ADOS orders that are found to exceed the standards of reference (j) will be placed on BCP by the GFC.

8. Service Limitations

a Marines are not eligible for ADOS orders that would result in AD service within 30 days of the individual's mandatory removal date, end of contract, or approved date of retirement in accordance with reference (g).

b. If necessary, enlisted Marines shall re-enlist prior to acceptance of orders in order to satisfy this requirement.

9. <u>Separations Pay Screening</u>. To ensure visibility and manage expectations regarding the potential payment of separations pay, all orders in MROWS in excess of five years of consecutive AD, including breaks of less than 31 days, will be screened by Director, MM (MMFA) for Contingency Operations (MPMC) funded orders, Director, MP (MPP-40) for MPMC funded orders, and Director, RA for RPMC funded orders.

10. <u>Additional Personnel Requirements</u>

    a. RC Marines must be satisfactory participants in the SMCR, IMA, or IRR.

    b. ADOS shall not be considered a substitute for annual unit training requirements.

    c. Marines desiring to perform ADOS shall clearly understand that the ADOS assignment is temporary and there is no entitlement, express or implied, for continued ADOS assignments, AD retirement, or other career incentives.

Program Administration

1. General. This enclosure provides detailed information on the orders writing, entitlements, administration, and release from AD for ADOS personnel.

2. Initiating Orders

    a. ADOS-AC and ADOS-RC

        (1) Individual Marines request orders via their parent command, GFC, or Operational Sponsor who will determine what type of orders meets the requirement: ADOS-AC, ADOS-RC, or ADOS-CO.

        (2) The gaining command must clearly articulate billet requirements, duties, special qualifications, experience necessary, level of security clearance, location of duty assignment, and the unit POC information in the orders request submission.

        (3) Commands may approve ADOS-AC and ADOS-RC up to 365 days, based on the ADOS budget provided via their respective Operational Sponsor and Director, RA.

        (4) Requests for ADOS orders shall be submitted via the chain of command to the appropriate funding source at least 30 days prior to the effective date.

        (5) Orders exceeding 365 days continuous AD (conventional ADOS), end strength exclusions, or five years continuous AD (including mobilization) require submission at least 60 days prior to the effective date for screening by DC M&RA.

        (6) Per reference (c), requests for orders which will result in the Marine exceeding 16 years of active service require submission at least 60 days in advance.

        (7) Upon approval, the orders writing authority will promptly issue orders to provide the member ample opportunity for employer notification or PCS coordination.

        (8) Additional requirements for ADOS-AC or ADOS-RC that exceed the previously budgeted amount for the command must be identified to Director, RA for approval.

    b. ADOS-CO. All requests for ADOS-CO orders must be routed through Director, MM (MMFA).

3. Orders to Active Duty

a. ADOS orders will be generated using the Marine Reserve Orders Writing System (MROWS).

b. In accordance with reference (h), Marines without official orders are not authorized to perform ADOS.

c. Requesting organizations are not authorized to bring an individual on AD without orders.

d. Commands without access to MROWS may request MROWS support from the next higher headquarters with MROWS capability.

e. If a request must be submitted manually, a NAVMC 11350 will be completed and forwarded via the chain of command.

f. ADOS requests for SMCR Marines will be submitted to the member's Commanding Officer/Officer-In-Charge/Inspector-Instructor.

g. Higher or adjacent commands interested in placing any SMCR or IMA on ADOS orders, from outside their parent command, are responsible for coordinating with the individual Marine's chain of command prior to issuing orders.

h. ADOS requests for Reserve General Officers will be submitted to Director, MM (MMSL).

i. Conventional ADOS is not a means to circumvent the Individual Augment (IA) or Service Augment (SA) approval processes when ADOS-CO orders would be more appropriate.

j. Per reference (l), ADOS-CO requests for IA's will be submitted to Director, MM (MMFA) at least 60 days prior to the effective date. Requests submitted less than 60 days prior to the effective date must provide justificiation as to why the 60 day window was not met.

k. Upon commencement and completion of the ADOS period, report the appropriate unit diary entries per references (h) and (m) and ensure that the correct component code is reported in MCTFS in accordance with reference (m) and enclosure (5).

l. Failure to properly identify the correct component code for the various types and duration of ADOS in MCTFS may misrepresent end strength accounting.

m. Contingency-related entitlements, to include education, income replacement, transitional health care, and other benefits are not authorized for members serving on conventional ADOS orders.

n. Commands requesting ADOS-AC (MPMC and O&MMC) will provide the orders writing authority with direct fund citation data to cover the travel and per diem costs.

o. If another Service provides this funding, the requesting command will also provide the contact information (address, phone) for the cognizant finance officer to facilitate settlement of travel upon completion of orders.

p. U.S. Marine Corps Forces (MARFORs) requesting ADOS-TSC orders will provide the issuing authority with the supported Combatant Commander direct fund citation data for travel and per diem purposes.

q. Funding for subsequent assignment of Reserve personnel to Temporary Additional Duty (TAD) while performing ADOS must be provided by the gaining command.

4. Pay and Entitlements

a. RC member pay, allowances, and entitlements, as prescribed by reference (n), are affected by ADOS tour length in accordance with reference (e).

b. Personnel assigned to ADOS for 180 days or less rate per diem, travel, and Basic Allowance for Housing (BAH), if otherwise entitled by the JFTR.

c. Assignments at one location may not exceed 180 consecutive days with per diem. The following stipulations apply:

(1) Personnel requesting orders with per diem beyond 180 consecutive days must take a 31-day break in between orders.

(2) In rare cases, per diem, in lieu of PCS orders in excess of 180 days, may be approved by DC M&RA.

(3) Requests for per diem in excess of 180 days require detailed justification of operational necessity and must be submitted to Director, MM (MMIA).

(4) Issuance of TAD orders for 180 days, with a break of less than 31 days, followed by another set of TAD orders at the same geographical location is not authorized if the known, or reasonbly anticipated, TAD duration was in excess of 180 days when the intitial order was issued.

d. Director, RA approval and tracking is required for conventional ADOS orders (other than for training) of 181 consecutive days or more. The following stipulations apply:

(1)   Per reference (e), members on Continental United States (CONUS) based ADOS-AC/RC orders of 181 consecutive days or more rate Permanent Change of Station (PCS) orders and are not entitled to per diem at the duty location, except while in a travel status.

(2) Per reference (e), members on Outside CONUS (OCONUS) based ADOS-AC/RC orders have differing PCS requirements based on country of destination. Appendix Q of reference (e) provides amplifying guidance related to PCS stipulations.

(3) Per reference (e), no-cost PCS orders may be authorized for ADOS executed within a reasonable commuting distance.

(4) Per reference (e), ADOS personnel executing PCS are authorized movement of household goods, temporary storage, and dependent travel.

e.   Family Separation Allowance (FSA) may be authorized for members on AD in excess of 30 days in accordance with reference (n) when dependent PCS travel is not authorized.

f.   Per reference (s), members on AD for 31 consecutive days or more must enroll in TRICARE Prime, while TRICARE standard coverage is automatically provided for the member's dependents.

(1) Members may elect to enroll dependents in TRICARE Prime or TRICARE Prime Remote (TPR).

(2) Enrollment of dependents in TRICARE Prime and TPR is based on the "20th of the month rule" for coverage to begin the 1st day of the following month.

g.   Per Section 12731 of reference (a), for AD service performed after 28 January 2008, the age a member is eligible to receive non-regular retired pay is reduced by three months from age 60 for every aggregate of 90 days of AD service performed within a FY.

h.   Per reference (n), "In Progress Payments" are paid to all Marines performing ADOS between 12 and 30 days.

i.   Additional ADOS-CO entitlements. Upon mobilization authority, DC M&RA (MMFA) will provide additional guidance regarding contingency operation entitlements. These include, but are not limited to the following:

(1) Per diem in excess of 180 days as authorized by SECNAV subject to restrictions established by DC M&RA (MMFA).

(2) TRICARE coverage up to 180 days prior to orders start date upon receipt of delayed-effective-date AD orders and 180 days after

orders termination date for Marines who complete at least 30 consecutive days of AD in support of contingency operations.

(3) Per reference (a), Chapter 1607, Reserve educational assistance is authorized.

5. Release from Active Duty

a. Because ADOS is a volunteer program, upon request, and subject to approval by the commander, Marines may terminate orders early with a minimum of two weeks notice given to the command.

b. Commanders may terminate a Marine's orders early, provided that the Marine is given a minimum of two weeks notice.

c. Reference (g) provides actions required of Marines separating upon conclusion of ADOS orders.

d. Marines performing ADOS orders of 31 days or more will have a NAVMC 11060, "Separation/Travel Pay Certificate", prepared by the Consolidated Personnel Administration Center (CPAC) or Installation Personnel Administration Center (IPAC) to direct separation payments.

Note: all Marines serving on ADOS-CO orders will receive a NAVMC 11060 for service that is greater than 24 hours.

e. Marines performing ADOS orders of 90 days or more will receive a DD214, "Certificate of Release or Discharge from Active Duty."

Note: all Marines on ADOS-CO will receive a DD214 for service that is greater than 24 hours.

f. Per reference (g), Marines performing more than six years of continuous AD service may be eligible for involuntary separation pay provided their "unqualified" written request for further AD was not approved by DC M&RA. Only those requests that specify that the member is willing to accept any assignment by the Commandant of the Marine Corps (CMC) will be considered "unqualified."

(1) Conventional ADOS. Submit an Administrative Action (AA) Form (NAVMC 10274) via the chain of command to Director, RA no less than six months prior to the orders termination date.

(2) ADOS-CO. Submit an AA form via the chain of command to Director, MM (MMFA) no less than six months prior to the orders termination date.

(3) If the Marine is denied further service, the servicing Personnel Administration Center (PAC) will submit the completed AA form as source documentation for payment of separation pay by the appropriate disbursing office in conjunction with the NAVMC 11060.

g. In accordance with references (n) and (u), leave accrued during ADOS will be accommodated within the term of the ADOS orders or may be sold back upon release from AD.

(1) Members serving on conventional ADOS may sell back accrued leave at the conclusion of their orders for periods of service in excess of 30 days up to 365 days without affecting the career cap of 60 days.

(2) Members serving on conventional ADOS in excess of 365 days who elect to sell back accrued leave at the conclusion of the period of ADOS will have such leave count against the career cap of 60 days.

(3) Members serving under ADOS-CO may sell back accrued leave at the conclusion of the period of ADOS-CO regardless of the duration of the orders without affecting the career cap of 60 days.

(4) Leave may be carried forward between consecutive orders provided there are no breaks of service greater than 24 hours.

(5) Per reference (h), extension of orders to execute accrued leave will not be approved.

h. Travel claims shall be liquidated in accordance with reference (e).

(1) Conventional ADOS Orders for 30 days or less will be settled by the Finance Office supporting the SMCR member's parent command. In the case of IMA and IRR Marines, the claims are settled by MFR/MOBCOM who retain administrative control of these personnel.

(2) Claims for orders exceeding 30 days are settled by the Finance Office serving the installation where the duty was performed.

Note: ADOS-CO orders are settled by the MOBCOM Finance Office.

(3) Claims for travel involving other Service or agency funding will be forwarded to the appropriate non-USMC finance office for settlement of associated travel and per diem.

(4) ADOS-CO partial and final travel claims must be submitted to the Marine Corps Reserve Activation Travel Section (MCRATS) under the Mobilization Command (MOBCOM) Finance Office.

i. Per reference (o), Reserve Marines in the grade of sergeant or above conducting ADOS require submission of fitness reports in accordance with the following criteria:

(1) SMCR members who have orders to perform ADOS away from their parent unit or under a different RS for 31 days or longer

require submission of a To Temporary Duty (TD) fitness report to cover the period from the end date of the Marine's last report to the day before the Marine goes to temporary duty.

(2) SMCR members completing a period of ADOS of 31 days or longer require a From Temporary Duty (FD) fitness report upon completion of the period of AD unless the reporting senior (RS) remains the same, in which case the RS is required to comment on the period of ADOS in the next reporting occasion.

(3) IRR Marines completing a period of ADOS of 31 days or longer require a Change of Status (CS) fitness report upon completion of the period of AD.

(4) Members of the SMCR and IRR completing a period of ADOS of 12-30 days require a Reserve Training (RT) fitness report. Reporting seniors may omit the RT report for reservists performing ADOS if they write the Marine's annual reserve report. When this occurs, the RS must include observations of the Marine's performance during annual Reserve training in the next reporting occasion. Section I directed comments apply.

j. Per reference (p), Marines in the grade of corporal or below completing ADOS orders of 31 days or greater require an ADOS RT proficiency and conduct marking upon being released from AD.

k. Physical Examination. Prior to being released from a period of AD, each Marine must complete a separation physical or medical release. The type of physical or medical release is contingent upon the duration of the period of duty and as set forth in paragraph (6) below.

6. Medical

a. Prior to serving on ADOS, the member must complete the medical requirements listed in enclosure (2) of this Order.

b. The member must sign the physical fitness certification resident in the orders acknowledging that the member is responsible for the accuracy of the fitness for duty statement under the UCMJ.

c. While on ADOS, it is the member's responsibility to report injuries via the chain of command as soon as they occur.

d. Prior to Completion of Active Duty

(1) Duty for 90 Days or Less

(a) A Marine on ADOS for 90 days or less should date and sign an SF-600 entry certifying that he or she did not incur any disabling injury or illness while on AD.

(b) Refusal to sign this statement will not delay separation.

(2) Duty Greater Than 90 Days

(a) A Marine on ADOS for a period of greater than 90 days must receive a complete medical examination prior to release from AD.

(b) Any changes in the member's physical condition should be appropriately annotated.

(c) Non-compliance with or scheduling delays in completing the pre-release physical shall not be the basis for a delay in the separation process.

e. Line of Duty

(1) Duty for Less Than 31 Days

(a) When a Marine is injured while on ADOS orders and the period of duty specified in the Marine's orders is less than 31 days, the Marine is required to be released from AD at the end of the orders period.

(b) Per reference (q), a Line of Duty (LOD) request must be submitted to CMC Wounded Warrior Regiment (WWR)/Reserve Medical Entitlements Determination (RMED) via the Marine Corps Medical Entitlements Data System (MCMEDS) to review, approve/disapprove, track, and manage LOD benefits throughout the Disability Evaluation System (DES) process.

(2) Duty for 31 days or more. Members injured while on ADOS orders in excess of 30 days whose injuries are not resolved before their EAS, and who elect to be released from AD vice being placed on medical hold, may request LOD benefits via their Reserve unit chain of command.

f. Medical Hold

(1) If a Marine incurs an illness or injury, or aggravates an existing injury, while on ADOS for 31 days or more and the member elects to be placed on medical hold, the command to which the Marine is assigned/attached will submit the request for medical hold to WWR.

(2) If approved by WWR all appropriate unit diary entries will be made in accordance with reference (m) by WWR.

(3) Because the funding and strength category changes when a Marine on ADOS is placed on medical hold, OpSponsors and gaining commands must inform the original order writing authority so they can

issue a modification to reflect accurate accounting of ADOS funds, operational support duty strength, and notify Director, RA.

(4) The effective date of the modification will be the date the Marine was placed on medical hold.

(5) If the original orders authorized per diem, per diem may continue while in a medical hold status.

(6) Marines on medical hold are not authorized to receive per diem in excess of 180 days without approval from DC M&RA (MMIA).

(7) Command Notification to WWR ensures proper tracking and disposition by a Medical Evaluation Board (MEB) and Physical Evaluation Board (PEB), if necessary.

(8) The Marine may choose to be separated and referred to the Veteran's Administration for treatment.

(9) Upon determination by a competent medical authority that the Marine is fit for duty, the original order writing authority and Director, RA must again be notified to terminate medical hold orders.

(10) If the Marine is unfit for duty, the Marine will be separated or medically retired in accordance with reference (g).

7. Legal

a. In accordance with reference (t), Marines on ADOS are subject to the UCMJ.

b. Jurisdiction

(1) The gaining commander has the authority to take legal action as authorized in the UCMJ with regard to a Reserve Marine on AD pursuant to ADOS orders.

(2) Authority to execute courts-martial and administer non-judicial punishment (NJP) is subject to the limitations contained in references (g), (h), (r), and (t).

c. Legal Hold

(1) A Reserve Marine on AD pursuant to ADOS may be placed on legal hold in accordance with reference (g).

(2) It is the responsibility of the gaining command to notify the Marine and run the appropriate unit diary entry indicating that the enlisted Marine is placed on legal hold.

(3) For officers, the gaining command is responsible for coordinating with their servicing MISSO to have the appropriate unit diary entry run.

(4) The pay group from which the orders are funded will not change when a Marine is placed on legal hold.

(5) The gaining command must inform the Operational Sponsor or parent command when a Marine serving on ADOS orders is placed on legal hold so that the Operational Sponsor may accurately account for their ADOS funds and initiate any required orders modifications.

d. A Marine may be involuntarily ordered to AD when an offense committed under the UCMJ is discovered after release from ADOS.

e. Per refernce (r), paragraph 0123, Officers exercising general courts-martial convening authority (GCMCA) have the authority to involuntary recall a Reserve Marine for NJP, Article 32 (UCMJ) investigation, or trial by court-martial if no confinement is being considered. When confinement is a consideration, the GCMCA may request that the Secretary of the Navy direct the involuntary recall of a Reserve Marine.

f. Involuntary recall orders will be funded by the gaining command using the same funding source in effect at the time the offense was committed.

8. <u>Training</u>. Marines performing ADOS for more than 30 days are required to conduct annual training with the gaining command unless otherwise exempted by the Commander.

ADOS Budget Working Group

1. <u>General</u>. The Director, RA is responsible for sponsoring the ADOS Budget Working Group (ABWG) meeting each FY to formulate and prioritize funding requirements for the current mid-year review and the upcoming budget submission for the next FY.

2. <u>Purpose</u>. This enclosure provides detailed information on the overarching authority, procedures, and conduct of the ABWG.

3. <u>Background</u>

    a. The ABWG is conducted annually during the 2nd Quarter of the FY.

    b. Organizations requiring ADOS support submit requirements and justifications annually in accordance with the ABWG convening MARADMIN.

    c. There are two functions of the ABWG.

        (1) To conduct a mid-year review of current FY.

        (2) To prioritize requirements and recommend allocation of anticipated funding for the upcoming FY to DC M&RA.

4. <u>Board Composition</u>. Voting members include the designated OpSponsors approved by DC M&RA and as delineated in the ABWG MARADMIN.

5. <u>Board Proceedings</u>

    a. <u>Current FY</u>

        (1) OpSponsors brief all remaining funds and unfunded requirements.

        (2) Prioritize all unfunded current year deficiencies.

        (3) Reallocate operational sponsor unplanned/unexecuted funds based upon prioritized current year deficiencies.

    b. <u>Subsequent FY</u>

        (1) OpSponsors brief command requirements for the upcoming FY.

        (2) Prioritize all requirements and tentatively allocate upcoming FY budget amounts based on anticipated funding.

    c. Forward ABWG recommended current and subsequent FY funding and prioritization to the Director, RA for approval or disapproval.

   d.   Submit remaining unfunded current/subsequent FY requirements
to DC P&R.

6.   <u>Program Manager Responsibilities (Director, RA)</u>

   a.   Prepare and release ABWG convening MARADMIN annually NLT 30
November.

   b.   Sponsor the ABWG annually during the 2nd Quarter of the FY.

   c.   Submit ABWG board results to the Director, Reserve Affairs for
approval/disapproval.

   d.   Prepare updated funding letters based upon reallocated funds.

   e.   Coordinate with DC P&R for potential additional allocations to
support unfunded current/subsequent FY deficiencies.

ADOS Categories and Component Codes

1. General. This enclosure provides detailed information on ADOS funding sources, budget execution categories, and subsequent component codes associated with the management of RC personnel serving on ADOS.

2. Funding Sources

a. Funding for ADOS is derived from the POM, Office of the Secretary of Defense transfers (e.g., counter drug operations), overseas contingency operation (OCO) sources, and congressional enhancements.

b. ADOS funding consists of MPMC, RPMC, and O&MMC appropriations (MROWS further delineates between Officer and Enlisted pay groups).

c. Members approved for separations pay will be funded by either RPMC or MPMC based on their last set of orders, regardless of the funding source for all previous orders.

d. ADOS-RC. The authority for ADOS-RC is derived from the RPMC budget with the purpose to provide Reserve personnel to short-term administrative, operational, and exercise support requirements that benefits the Reserves. Funding for this category includes pay and allowances, travel and per diem.

e. ADOS-AC. The authority for ADOS-AC is derived from the MPMC and O&MMC budgets with the purpose to provide Reserve personnel to short-term administrative, operational, and exercise support requirements that benefits the Active Component, with the exception of ADOS-CO orders.

(1) ADOS-AC funding consists of pay and allowances.

(2) O&MMC funding provides travel and per diem allowances.

f. ADOS-CO.

(1) The authority for ADOS-CO is based on duty in support of a contingency and is normally budgeted through OCO funding sources.

(2) This ADOS category consists of pay and allowances that are derived from the MPMC budget as well as O&MMC funded travel and per diem.

3. Budget Execution Categories. These categories are defined by DC P&R with specific expenditure attributes that support individual elements that make up the whole funding support package for the Marine Corps Reserve.

a. Reference (a), Section 115 further defines the parameters for ADOS use to support special projects, exercise related functions and emerging, unplanned requirements.

b. The nine RPMC budget execution categories include the following:

(1) <u>Drug Interdiction Activity</u>. Provides intelligence support, augmentation of the RC on Commander Navy Reserve Forces (CNRF) Frigates, and flight hours of Reserve Maritime Patrol Aircraft (VP) and Light Helicopter Anti-Submarine (HSL) counter-narcotics detection and monitoring operations in the SOUTHCOM and Joint Interagency Task Force (JIATF) AORs.

(2) <u>Exercises</u>. Provides for RC participation in Joint Chiefs of Staff directed and coordinated training exercises. Also included are field training exercises and command post exercises.

(3) <u>Command/Staff Supervision and Conferences</u>. Provides for command/staff inspection and supervision visits made by higher headquarters to subordinate units. The effectiveness of training and unit's capability to respond to wartime tasking is evaluated and compliance with directives is checked. Tours also provide for pre-annual training coordination conferences.

(4) <u>Management Support</u>. Includes support of those managerial and administrative tasks performed in support of projects directly related to training and administration of Marine Corps Reserve activities. Examples are promotion boards, development of instructional materials, exercise planning, training conferences and development of Marine Corps Reserve policies.

(5) <u>Operational Training</u>. Provides training directly related to probable wartime tasking. This includes training of an operational nature similar to that performed during IDT and AT. Also provides Reserve maintenance teams to perform on-site maintenance for supported units and Reserve air crews for Reserve Air/Ground exercises and Reserve troop lifts.

(6) <u>Service Mission/Mission Support</u>. Includes training, both unit and individual, which accomplishes a specific mission or task, or supports a specified mission or task for any of the Armed Services, as well as RC support of AC missions and internal support rendered to RC units and agencies.

(7) <u>Recruitment and Retention</u>. These tours provide for the ordering of Reservists to AD to augment the Regular recruiting force for purposes of recruiting non-prior service individuals for the Selected Marine Corps Reserve.

(8) <u>Competitive Events</u>. Provides for participation and support of individuals in competitive events to include marksmanship, Olympic Championships and trials, and the annual Confederation of Inter-allied Reserve Officers (abbreviated as CIOR) Championships and Pentathlon events.

    (9) <u>Military Funeral Honors</u>. Provides for RC participation in rendering of military funeral honors for veterans.